living in berlin

living in berlin

Federico Ferrari

Motta Architettura

Edited and published by
24 ORE Cultura srl, Milano

english translation
Sylvia Adrian Notini

cover
Deadline > office for architectural
services, Bender, Berlin, 2003-2004,
photo by Matthew Griffin, Berlin

First Edition
April 2010

ISBN 978-88-6116-121-4

Abitare a Berlino: nuovi spazi per nuovi stili di vita

A nemmeno vent'anni dalla caduta del Muro, Berlino ha assunto il ruolo di capitale culturale europea. Un laboratorio di nuovi stili di vita, dall'atmosfera cosmopolita e vivace, ben lontana dall'aspetto fatiscente e malinconico che contraddistingueva la città sino al 1989. Il passato è in realtà diventato volano per il futuro: ciò che colpisce il visitatore di questa metropoli del XXI secolo è la sensazione di trovarsi di fronte a una città di frammenti ricomposti. Le ferite della storia sono insomma diventate un'occasione per ripartire con nuovo slancio verso un avvenire in cui l'architettura ha assunto un ruolo di primo piano. L'*exploit* edilizio ha suggellato la riunificazione attraverso una serie infinita di grandi opere pubbliche, i cui autori, da Renzo Piano con l'intervento di Potsdamer Platz a Norman Foster, con la riqualificazione del glorioso Reichstag, il più delle volte hanno operato ricucendo un organismo urbano altrimenti frantumato. L'eredità del passato ha infatti costituito un punto di partenza ineludibile, non solo per le *archistar* che hanno ripensato l'immagine pubblica della nuova capitale, ma anche per la miriade di piccoli o medi interventi residenziali distribuiti sulla sconfinata superficie metropolitana.

Berlino è infatti da sempre una mostra permanente di architettura. Oltre alle emergenze monumentali, che dal XVIII secolo, quando la piccola città sulle rive della Sprea assurge a simbolo della potenza prussiana, punteggiano l'Unter den Linden, anche il tema residenziale ha rappresentato, soprattutto a partire dagli inizi del Novecento, un classico campo di sperimentazione. È in quegli anni che la cultura razionalista ha tentato di inverare l'utopia di una società armonicamente regolata, di cui l'architettura doveva essere allo stesso tempo metafora e presupposto. Se infatti, sino alla fine dell'Ottocento, la residenza borghese nei quartieri centrali e le *Mietskasernen* operaie – i complessi intensivi con cui la cultura urbanistica aveva tentato di ovviare alla cronica carenza di alloggi delle masse inurbate – nella cintura periferica, traducevano architettonicamente le rigide gerarchie sociali allora imperanti, nel XX secolo diventa chiaro come tale modello non sia più sostenibile. Dapprima, sino alla caduta del Reich guglielmino, si assiste a sperimentazioni frammentarie e pionieristiche, ma, con l'avvento della repubblica di Weimar, l'iniziativa statale e la nuova coscienza delle élite intellettuali individuano nella qualità dell'abitare il presupposto fondamentale di una società democratica. Il convergere della nuova cultura architettonica razionalista, i cui maggiori protagonisti – fra gli altri, Walter Gropius, Mies van der Rohe, Bruno Taut, Erich Mendelsohn – hanno proprio in Germania la loro patria, e del mutato quadro politico dominato almeno per un decennio dal modello socialdemocratico, determinano quella miscela esplosiva che farà di Weimar uno straordinario – seppur tormentato – laboratorio della modernità. E Berlino non poteva che essere lo specchio di questo tentativo di sperimentazione sociale, alla cui base, almeno nei primi anni dopo la guerra, stava un'incoercibile entusiasmo per il futuro e, di converso, un'altrettanto radicale volontà di chiudere con il passato. La Berlino di quegli anni è infatti una città secolare, ricca di storia e cultura, diventata improvvisamente simbolo di modernità, anticonformismo e babele dei linguaggi assunta a emblema di libertà e pluralismo.

Non deve dunque sorprendere che la cifra distintiva della metropoli tedesca sia ancor oggi la continua capacità di reinventare se stessa. Dopo la rovinosa caduta del totalitarismo nazista, il Muro contribuirà a cristallizzare, per più di quarant'anni, le ferite della storia fattesi macerie, inverando nell'architettura la catastrofe di un intero popolo. Il risultato sarà un tessuto urbano quanto mai poroso e slabbrato, proprio di una città in cui non esisterà più un vero centro e in cui interi isolati sopravviveranno, sin nel cuore di Mitte, come "vuoti" anonimi e disabitati. Senza considerare la natura di queste "lacune urbane" non è possibile comprendere la colossale operazione di riconfigurazione avviata nel 1989, e nemmeno, per quanto riguarda i luoghi dell'abitare dell'ultimo decennio protagonisti di questa pubblicazione, le originali tipologie residenziali che hanno costituito uno dei principali tasselli della ricucitura urbana realizzata a partire dagli anni Novanta. La presenza diffusa di ampie porzioni di suolo libero rende infatti del tutto peculiare la situazione berlinese. Basti pensare che attualmente Berlino conta all'incirca 3.500.000 abitanti, distribuiti su una superficie che è grosso modo analoga all'estensione della metropoli alla fine della seconda guerra mondiale, quando la capitale del Reich contava ben 4.500.000 residenti. La densità è insomma infinitamente più bassa rispetto a quella di analoghe metropoli occidentali e di conseguenza le nuove edificazioni non corrispondono ad aree d'espansione, ma si collocano su ampie porzioni di suolo libero all'interno della città consolidata. È noto infatti che a Berlino le abitazioni costano in media la metà rispetto alle altre capitali europee. La nozione di periferia cui solitamente si fa ricorso nella gran parte dei contesti urbani è dunque assai inappropriata.

La porosità dell'edificato è stata decisiva per consentire l'esplosione di innumerevoli micro iniziative architettoniche, corrispondenti al crogiuolo di stili di vita e nuovi *trend* culturali che contraddistinguono il tessuto sociale berlinese. La flessibilità e l'eterogeneità sono gli imperativi di gran parte dell'edilizia residenziale sorta negli ultimi anni. Di conseguenza l'ibridismo è la cifra distintiva delle tipologie abitative: gli Höfe di Mitte – in gran parte collocati su Oranienburger

Straße – corti storiche divenute luoghi del tempo libero integrati a residenza medio-borghese, convivono con i palazzi per uffici sorti su Friedrichstraße e con edifici industriali dismessi, che ancora portano i segni della guerra e spesso sono stati colonizzati da giovani artisti emergenti. In altri casi, edifici produttivi hanno subito radicali riconversioni, trasformandosi in *loft* per giovani coppie o single.

I quartieri dell'ex capitale della DDR scampati alle devastazioni della guerra, primo fra tutti Prenzlauer Berg, sono rinati a nuova vita grazie all'"invasione" della folta comunità straniera, richiamata a Berlino dai prezzi estremamente favorevoli e dalle molteplici opportunità di lavoro. Neukölln o Kreuzberg, quartieri multietnici dominati dalla presenza della cospicua comunità turca, da zone degradate e marginali della ex Berlino Ovest si sono tramutati in aree alternative, attraverso il recupero, spesso in modo informale, della superstite edilizia ottocentesca. Eclatante è il caso di Mahrzan, desolato e decentrato quartiere dell'ex Est, situato a dieci chilometri da Alexander Platz: accanto ai tradizionali abitanti convivono oggi schiere di giovani della più varia estrazione, che hanno fatto di quest'anonima porzione di città il teatro della scena *underground*. È in questi casi che si può osservare come gli spazi anonimi e irrisolti, a contatto con l'energia spontanea e irriverente delle culture giovanili desiderose di sperimentare nuovi stili di vita, esprimano al meglio tutto il proprio potenziale creativo. Non è scampata a questa logica del riuso nemmeno l'arcigna edilizia socialista di stato. Riconvertite, le alte stecche *moderniste* nei dintorni di Alexander Platz e di Hackescher Markt, oltre che i complessi intensivi a sud di Karl-Marx-Allee, hanno potuto soddisfare una pressante domanda abitativa. Un esempio estremo di quest'abilità nel riconferire vitalità urbana anche a oggetti apparentemente estranei alla cultura dell'abitare è senza dubbio quello della nuova Berlin Bunker Gallery: nel severo volume in cemento armato di un bunker costruito nel 1942 ha trovato posto la Sammlung Boros Collection e all'ultimo piano, in una serie di corpi aggiunti, l'abitazione del collezionista, circondata da terrazze affacciate su Mitte e sul cuore commerciale e finanziario di Friedrichstraße. I volumi giustapposti in modo irriverente sulla sommità del bunker sono certamente la metafora più compiuta di un ibridismo capace di conciliare un forte rispetto della memoria con un'affermazione altrettanto decisa di forme e stili schiettamente contemporanei. Altro esempio interessante di commistione fra passato e futuro è rappresentato dalla Lofthaus di Marcus Coelen, ricavata in un ex edificio commerciale dai candidi prospetti. Per quanto riguarda invece la pratica tipicamente berlinese di saturare l'interno degli isolati riconvertendo edifici produttivi, occorre menzionare l'intervento di Margit Kleibaum Freischaffende Architektin in Kastanienallee.

Come si diceva, Berlino è anche città di grandi spazi vuoti. Oltre agli innumerevoli parchi, polmoni verdi distribuiti omogeneamente sull'intera superficie urbana, l'edificato, almeno fino a pochi anni fa, era ancora eroso dal depositarsi delle ferite della storia. Il turbinio di riqualificazioni dell'esistente è andato dunque di pari passo con la saturazione di questi "vuoti urbani", nel tentativo di riconferire compattezza al tessuto edilizio. Naturalmente, le zone un tempo solcate dal Muro sono state le prime a essere interessate dalla riedificazione, in un processo colossale culminato con l'operazione ad alto valore simbolico di Potsdamer Platz. Tuttavia, allontanandosi dai luoghi più noti, è interessante notare come le operazioni qualitativamente migliori si siano svolte intervenendo su piccoli lotti, dove l'edilizia residenziale ha assolto un fondamentale ruolo di ricomposizione degli isolati. È in questi casi che si può apprezzare al meglio la varietà di tipologie che punteggiano la città, direttamente corrispondenti alle molteplici esigenze di un tessuto sociale quanto mai cangiante. Esse sono riassumibili in gran parte in tre categorie: edifici a cortina, edifici multipiano a blocco isolato e case unifamiliari o a schiera. Gli edifici a cortina svolgono in tal senso un compito fondamentale di ricucitura: fra i tanti, il trasparente fabbricato d'angolo di Nägeliarchitekten, la scomposta facciata a pannelli di Angelis + Partner Architekten, il piccolo ma prezioso intervento di Ebers-Architekten, la flessibile facciata a griglie scorrevoli di Abcarius & Burns e il disarticolato volume di Grüntuch Ernst Architekten BDA. Una menzione particolare merita l'edificio in Pappelallee di Stefan Tebroke con Carlo Calderan: situato nel cuore di Prenzlauer Berg, le ristrette dimensioni del lotto sono diventate l'occasione per articolare la facciata con una serie di ampie aperture quadrangolari, funzionali alla eterogeneità di tagli abitativi presenti all'interno. Allontanandosi dalle zone più densamente edificate è tuttavia frequente incontrare anche tipologie più tradizionali. In questi casi assume un ruolo decisivo la presenza del verde privato o semi-pubblico, spazio di connessione per eccellenza in una città dalla forte sensibilità ecologista. Numerosi progetti recenti hanno indagato le potenzialità del blocco isolato multipiano. Oltre alle zone più periferiche, non mancano esempi in tal senso anche all'interno degli isolati centrali. È il caso degli imponenti volumi dei Parkside Apartments di David Chipperfield, così come dei sobri blocchi modulari di Kny & Weber Architekten. Le *Stadtvillen* di Franz Schmid Freischaffender Architekt sono invece una tipologia ibrida: concepiti come diversi corpi indipendenti, ognuno di essi assomma in sé quattro tagli differenti di appartamenti, la cui articolazione si riverbera nelle facciate mosse e terrazzate.

Secondo una tradizione tipicamente nordica, sono numerosi anche gli esempi di abitazioni unifamiliari o a schiera, tipologie anch'esse appropriate a esplorare nuove e più flessibili forme di vita. Fra le tante realizzazioni occorre menzionare la vibratile Haus Dichter di Katharina Müller-Stüler, l'algido cubo traforato di ARGE Bonnen + Schlaich, la plastica Giebelhäuser dal tetto ricurvo di Nägeliarchitekten, la metafisica villa unifamiliare di Alexander Gyalokay e Heike Schley, la raffinata casa "a lamelle" di Anne Kleinlein e la discreta e smaterializzata Haus smac di Kleyer.Koblitz.Architekten e Julia Bergmann.

A testimonianza dell'estrema flessibilità dell'isolato berlinese nell'accogliere le sperimentazioni più radicali è da citare il progetto dell'Urban Village di Martashof. Un grande isolato nel cuore di Prenzlauer Berg accoglierà nel 2010 diverse unità immobiliari: dal *single flat* di circa 60 mq ai 165 mq della casa su tre livelli, corredati da giardini interni, terrazze-giardino e patii. Caratteristica innovativa di questo intervento è la possibilità di "creare" il proprio spazio abitativo, personalizzandone il numero di stanze, il layout e la struttura (in orizzontale o in verticale).

Un altro elemento qualificante di Berlino è la costante presenza dell'acqua. I grandi parchi pubblici, oltre a costituire zone cuscinetto fra quartieri dalle forti specificità identitarie, hanno il loro contrappunto nel dedalo di fiumi, canali e bacini lacustri, che soprattutto in estate animano il tessuto urbano. Pur lontana dal mare e dalle spiagge baltiche, a Berlino l'acqua ha infatti assunto un ruolo ben al di là del puro dato paesaggistico-ornamentale. Essa è diventata spunto per sperimentare innovative soluzioni residenziali, come testimoniano numerosi progetti e realizzazioni. È il caso delle ventiquattro case-barca posizionate lungo la Sprea, l'Havel, il bacino di Spandau e la baia di Rummelsburg, che, ancorate a pontoni lungo la riva, sono state disposte a gruppi di due o quattro unità. Assieme ai numerosi barconi-bar che punteggiano diversi altri canali, come il celebre Kreuz Kanal tra Neukölln e Kreuzberg, esse possono essere considerate simbolo di nuovi modi di concepire la vita urbana.

Dagli appartamenti per single a quelli per giovani coppie, dalle "comuni" alle residenze di giovani artisti, spesso integrate con laboratori e atelier, dagli ostelli alle abitazioni per il più classico dei nuclei familiari – che trovano a Berlino un habitat decisamente "a misura di bambino" – l'eterogeneità delle culture e dei modi di vita ha avuto dunque un effetto dirompente sull'edilizia della nuova capitale tedesca. É forse dunque l'immagine dell'acqua a descrivere nel modo più vivido questa realtà "liquida" e cangiante, alla ricerca costante di stili di vita alternativi fra nomadismo e libertà.

Federico Ferrari

Living in Berlin: new spaces for new lifestyles

It hasn't been twenty years since the Wall fell and the city of Berlin is already shouldering the role of cultural capital of the world: a veritable laboratory of new lifestyles, with an atmosphere at once cosmopolitan and exciting, a far cry from the run-down and forlorn air that once distinguished the city, until the year 1989. But the truth is that the past has actually had a flywheel effect on the future, and the visitor of this 21st-century metropolis soon has the impression of standing before a city of reassembled pieces. In short, the scars left by history have turned into an opportunity to start over again, and with great élan, towards a future where the role of architecture comes to the fore. The great effort to rebuild has corroborated German reunification through an endless series of great public works, whose authors, from Renzo Piano and his redevelopment of Potsdamer Platz, to Norman Foster and his transformation of the glorious Reichstag, have in most instances laboured by stitching back together an urban organism otherwise shattered. The legacy from the past has provided an inescapable point of departure, and not just for all the "archistars" who have reflected on a public image for the new capital, but for the myriad residential constructions of small to medium dimension stretching throughout the boundless metropolitan surface, as well.

Berlin has really always been a permanent exhibition of architecture. Alongside the monuments that have dotted the Unter den Linden since the 18th century, when a small city on the banks of the River Spree sprang up to symbolize Prussian rule, the building of homes has likewise forever been an area open to experimentation, especially from the early 20th century. Those were the years when Rationalist culture endeavoured to make true the utopia of a society characterized by harmonious order, for which architecture was to be both metaphor and presupposition. If, in fact, until the end of the 19th century, bourgeois residence in the city's central quarters, and the working class Miets-kasernen in the outskirts – densely populated tenement complexes which urban culture had attempted to use to make up for the chronic lack of housing for the urbanized masses – were the architectural translation of the rigid social hierarchies in rule at the time, in the 20th century it was soon evident that a model of the kind was no longer sustainable. Although some fragmentary and early experimentation did take place in the years leading up to the fall of the Wilhelmine Reich, it was not until the Weimar Republic that government initiative and the new awareness of the intellectual élite began to view quality of living as the underlying requirement for any democratic society. The convergence between a new Rationalist architectural culture, whose most eminent protagonists – Walter Gropius, Mies van der Rohe, Bruno Taut, Erich Mendelsohn, to name only a few – were themselves German-born, and the new political scene, which had been dominated for at least a decade by the Social Democrat model, determined the explosive combination that would make Weimar an extraordinary – albeit tormented – laboratory of modernity. And Berlin was nothing short of the reflection of this endeavour to experiment socially, at the basis of which, at least in the first years after the war, lay an incoercibile enthusiasm for the future, but also a radical desire to put an end to the past. The Berlin of those years was, in fact, a secular city, rich in history and culture, which had suddenly become a symbol of modernity, anticonformism and a babel of languages - a city chosen to be the emblem of freedom and pluralism.

It should therefore come as no surprise that this German city's distinctive trait continues to be its skill at reinventing itself. For more than forty years after the ruinous fall of Nazi totalitarianism, the Wall would contribute to crystallizing the wounds of history that were now nothing more than debris, with architecture as visual proof of the catastrophe of an entire people. The outcome of this was a vastly porous and deformed urban texture, that of a city where a real centre no longer existed, and in which entire blocks would survive as anonymous and uninhabited "voids" all the way into the heart of Mitte. Any attempt to overlook the nature of these "urban gaps" would mean failure to grasp the colossal operation to redesign the city begun in 1989; it would also mean not fully understanding – in regard to the housing of the past ten years and the subject of this publication – the original residential typologies, so crucial to the urban mending that was implemented from the nineties. What is unique about Berlin is the presence of vast, empty sites. Suffice it to recall that Berlin currently counts approximately 3,500,000 inhabitants distributed over a surface area that is more or less equal to the total area for the city at the end of the Second World War, when the residents of the capital of the Reich numbered as many as 4,500,000. In short, the population density here is infinitely less than that of similar western capitals, and what this means is that its new buildings do not correspond to areas of expansion, but are, rather, scattered over broad portions of empty sites within the consolidated city. The price for a house in Berlin is known to be on the average half of what it is in other European capitals, and the notion of the "outskirts" which is generally applied to urban contexts is inappropriate here.

Of crucial importance to the explosion of countless architectural micro-initiatives, all of which corresponding to the melting-pot of lifestyles and new cultural trends distinctive of Berlin's social texture, was the fact that the city's built-up area could actually be penetrated. And the majority of the residential buildings that have gone up in recent years are insistently characterized by flexibility and diversity. The distinctive trait of the city's residential typologies is therefore a hybrid structure: the Mitte district's Höfe - historical courtyards turned leisure-time locations integrated with housing for the middle-class, most of which located on Oranienburger Straße - cohabit with the office buildings that have sprung up on Friedrichstraße, as well as with abandoned industrial buildings that still bear the scars of war and are often colonized by young, emerging artists. In other cases still, productive buildings have undergone radical conversions, and been transformed into lofts for young couples or singles. The districts of the former capital of the GDR that managed to survive the destruction of war, a foremost example being Prenzlauer Berg, have been granted a new life, thanks to the "invasion" of a huge community of foreigners attracted to Berlin because of its affordable prices and numerous work opportunities. Neukölln or Kreuzberg, multiethnic suburbs dominated by the presence of conspicuous Turkish communities, and at one time former West Berlin's marginal areas of urban blight, are now transfigured into alternative areas via the often informal recovery of still-standing 19th-century constructions. Particularly impressive is the case of Mahrzan, a deserted and decentralized district in what was once the East, located ten kilometres from Alexander Platz; side by side with its traditional inhabitants are flocks of young people from a panoply of extractions who have turned this anonymous part of the city into a theatre for the underground scene - proof that when anonymous and unresolved spaces come into contact with the spontaneous and irreverent energy of youth cultures eager to experiment with new lifestyles, they, too, end up expressing every bit of their own creative potential. Nor has the state's gloomy socialist architecture been able to escape this logic of reutilization. Also contributing to satisfying the great demand for housing, after their conversion, are the tall modernist highrises located near Alexander Platz and Hackescher Markt, as well as the dense complexes south of Karl-Marx-Allee. Undoubtedly an extreme example of this skill at restoring urban vitality to objects which might otherwise appear to be extraneous to the culture of living is the new Berlin Bunker Gallery: once a stern reinforced concrete air-raid shelter built in 1941, this private gallery now accomodates the Sammlung Boros Collection, and at the very top, after several interventions, the collector's penthouse surrounded by balconies overlooking Mitte and the business and financial heart of Friedrichstraße.

Visible at the top of the bunker are several volumes that have been irreverently juxtaposed there, the perfect metaphor for a hybridism capable of reconciling an unwavering respect for memory with an equally resilient affirmation of straightforwardly contemporary forms and styles. Another fascinating example of past and future combined is the Lofthaus designed by Marcus Coelen, made from a former light-façaded commercial building. An example, instead, of the typically Berlinese practice of saturating the inner portions of blocks by converting buildings once used for produtive purposes is the work of Margit Kleibaum Freischaffende Architektin on Kastanienallee.

But as I was saying, Berlin is also the city of great empty spaces. In addition to its numerous parks - green lungs evenly distributed over the entire urban surface - until a few years ago, the city's built-up area was still eroded by the scars of war that seemed to have permanently settled there. Nonetheless, the flurry to requalify what was already there went hand in hand with the saturation of these "urban voids", in the attempt to restore compactness to the built-up portions of the city. The areas where the Wall had once stood were, of course, the first to be involved in efforts to rebuild, part of a colossal process which culminated with the highly symbolic redevelopment of Potsdamer Platz. But if we move away from famous locations it's interesting to note how the finest redevelopment, qualitatively speaking, came about in small lots, where residential architecture took on the fundamental role of putting the blocks back together. Here is where one may truly appreciate the variety of typologies dotting the city, and directly corresponding to the multiple needs of an ever-changing social texture. Most of these are classified as belonging to one of three categories: high-density brick-faced buildings, multi-storey buildings in an isolated block, and single-family dwellings or terraced houses. Brick-faced buildings play a crucial role in the task of patching things up, and the city's numerous examples include: the transparent corner building by Nägeliarchitekten, the façade of uneven panelling by Angelis + Partner Architekten, the small but precious intervention by Ebers-Architekten, the flexible façade made of sliding grids by Abcarius & Burns and, lastly, the volume designed by Grüntuch Ernst Architekten BDA which features a repeating break in continuity. Especially deserving of mention is the building on Pappelallee designed by Stefan Tebroke with Carlo Calderan: situated in the heart of Prenzlauer Berg, the narrow dimensions of the lot have suggested using a series of wide quadrangular openings to modulate the façade, which are functional to the diversity of the types of units present inside.

Moving away from the densest areas of construction more traditional typologies are observed, where an all-important role is played by the presence of private or semi-public green spaces, the quintessential connecting network for a city that feels very strongly about ecology. Numerous recent projects have investigated the potential of the multi-storey isolated block, visible in the city's outer areas as well as in the centre. Examples are the impressive volumes of David Chipperfield's Parkside Apartments, and the sober modular blocks by Kny & Weber Architekten. The Stadtvillen by Franz Schmid Freischaffender Architekt are instead a hybrid typology: conceived of as several independent constructs, each of these accomodates four different types of flats, whose design reverberates in the animated, balconied façades.

Reminiscent of Nordic tradition are the numerous examples of single-

family or terraced houses, typologies also suited to exploring new, more flexible lifestyles. Among the many, mention must be made of the vibratile Haus Dichter designed by Katharina Müller-Stüler, the cold cube with openwork by ARGE Bonnen + Schlaich, the plastic Giebelhäuser with its sloping roof plane by Nägeliarchitekten, the metaphysical single-family home by Alexander Gyalokay and Heike Schley, the refined "thin-plated" house by Anne Kleinlein and, lastly, the discreet and dematerialized Haus smac designed by Kleyer. Koblitz.Architekten and Julia Bergmann.

Proof of the extreme versatility of the Berlinese block in welcoming even the most radical of experiments in housing is the project for the Martashof Urban Village, a vast block in the heart of Prenzlauer Berg which in 2010 will accomodate a variety of residential units: from the single 60-square-metre flat to the 165-square-metre three-storey house complete with inner gardens, balcony-gardens and patios. One of the project's most innovative features is the opportunity it offers to "create" one's own living space, personalizing the number of rooms, layout and structure (horizontal or vertical).

Further qualifying the city of Berlin is the water visible everywhere. Public parks acting as buffer zones between strongly identity-oriented areas of the city contrast with the maze of rivers, canals and lake basins that enliven the urban texture, especially so in summer. Although far from the sea and the Baltic shores, water in Berlin has in fact taken on a role that goes much beyond that of mere ornament for the landscape, and become the point of departure for experiments conducted on innovative residential solutions in numerous projects and other initiatives. The twenty-four houseboats positioned all along the Rivers Spree and Havel, the basin of water at Spandau and the bay at Rummelsburg are a case in point; anchored to pontoons situated all along the shore these houseboats are arranged in groups of two or four units, and together with the numerous bar-barges that speckle the other canals - the famed Kreuz Kanal between Neukölln and Kreuzberg, for instance - they symbolize a new way of thinking about urban life.

From apartments for singles to homes for young couples, from "communes" to the houses of young artists, often integrated with workshops and studios, from hostels to the most traditional of houses for families – which discover Berlin to be an unquestionably "child-friendly" habitat – this mixture of cultures and lifestyles has had a powerful effect on the new German capital's building activity. Perhaps the image of water is the best way to describe this "free-flowing", changing reality, this constant quest for alternative lifestyles poised somewhere between wanderlust and freedom.

Federico Ferrari

living in berlin

Urbane Living 2

abcarius+burns
architecture design

year	2004
photos	Ludger Paffrath
site	www.abcariusburns.de

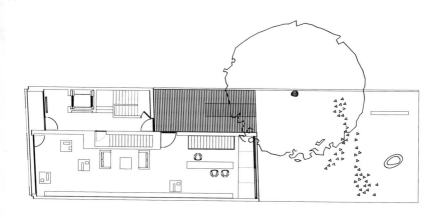

0 1   5 m

+ 2

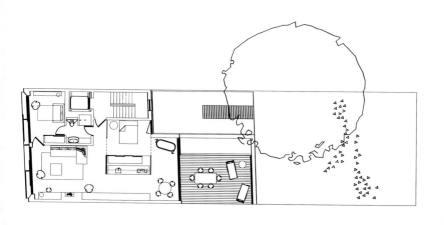

+ 3

Zeimer House   AFF architekten

year	2006
photos	Sven Fröhlich
site	www.aff-architekten.com

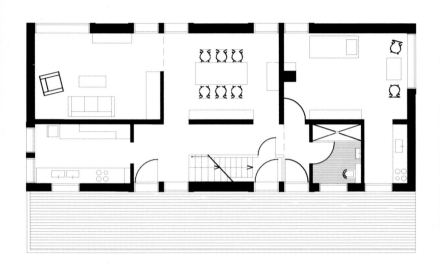

0   1   3 m

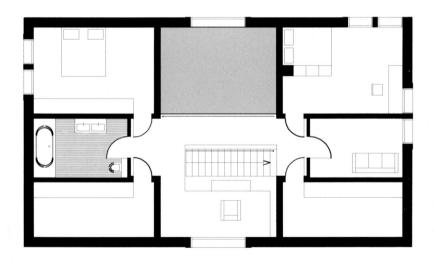

Apartment and Office Building

ANGELIS+PARTNER Architekten

year	2006
address	Alte Schönhauser Straße 42
collaborators	ANGELIS+PARTNER Architekten: Alexis Angelis, Gregor Angelis, Manfred Delor, Joachim Finke, Horst Gumprecht, Claus Nannen, Linn Voss, Kathrin Bockholt, Peter Haslinger, Carolin Bornhorst, Irek Gaszyna; Jürgen Hellmann (structural engineering), Donker&Dammann (technical engineering)
photos	Werner Huthmacher
site	www.angelis-partner.de

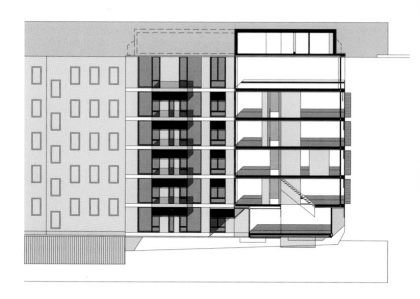

0 2   10 m

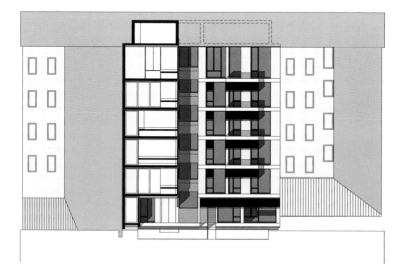

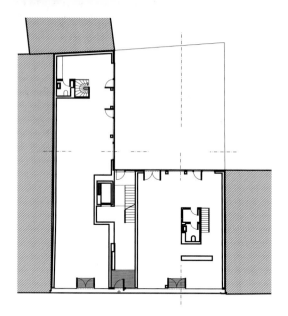

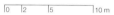

0   2   5   10 m

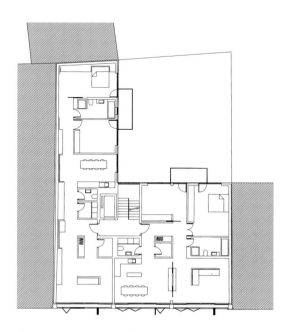

+ 1

Three Artists' Studios in Königsweg

Becher Rottkamp

year	2000
collaborators	Gesellschaft von Architekten (general planner)
photos	Stefan Müller
site	www.becher-rottkamp.de

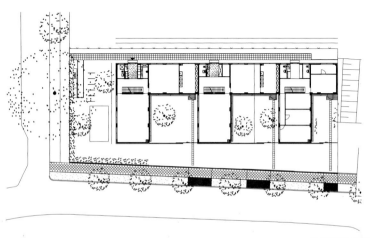

0   5   15 m

Detached Residence at Priesterberg

Oliver Collignon, Collignon Architektur

year	1996
address	Am Priesterberg 10
collaborators	Gabriella Pape (landscape designer),
	Arup (structural & domestic engineering),
	Licht Kunst Licht (lighting design)
photos	Jens Willebrand
site	www.collignonarchitektur.com

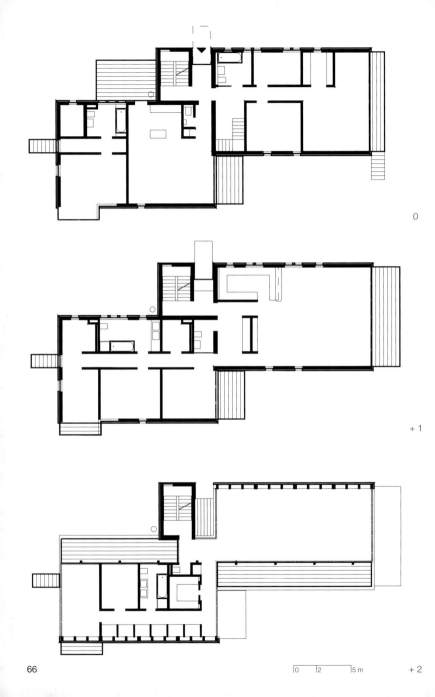

0

+ 1

0   2   5 m

+ 2

Bender

Deadline > office for architectural services .

year	2003-2004
address	Hessische Straße 5
collaborators	Britta Jürgens, Matthew Griffin, Stefan Bullerkotte, Kristine Verdier, Hans Christian Wilhelm
photos	Matthew Griffin
site	www.deadline.de

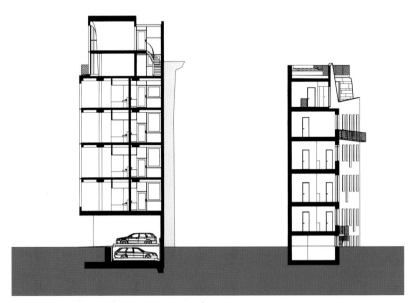

0 2   10 m

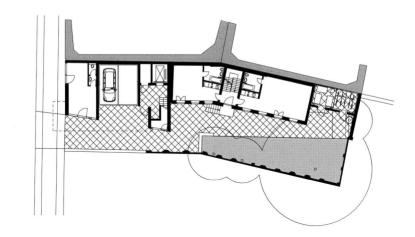

0   2   10 m

0

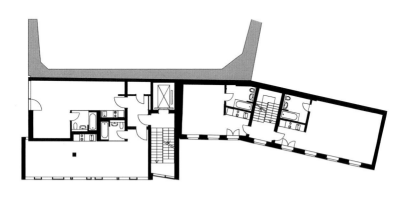

80

+ 1

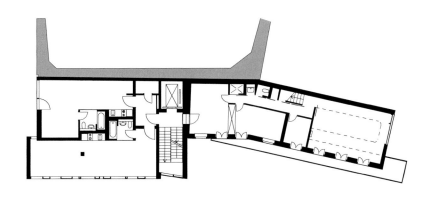

+ 3

0 2   10 m

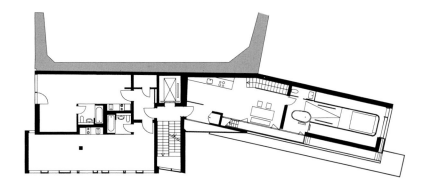

+ 4

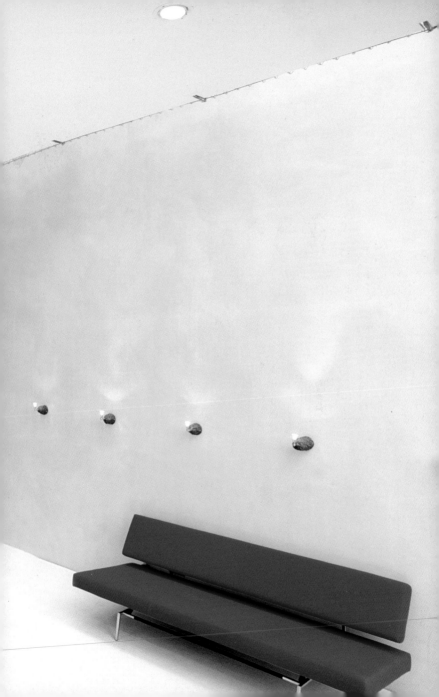

City House in Auguststraße 26a

joerg ebers architekt

year	2004-2005
address	Auguststraße 26a
collaborators	Daniel Buchheit
photos	Ulrich Schwarz
site	www.ebers-architekten.de

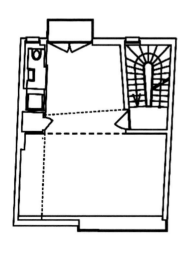

+ 1

+ 2

0 |1 |5 m

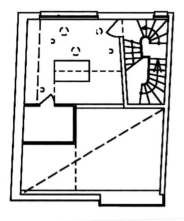

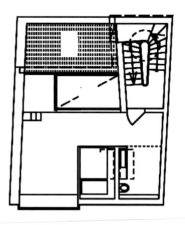

+ 3

+ 4

93

Residence in Berlin-Mahlsdorf

Alexander Gyalokay, Heike Schley

year	2005
address	Majakowskiring 67/69
photos	Alexander Gyalokay, Heike Schley
site	www.gyalokay-schley.de

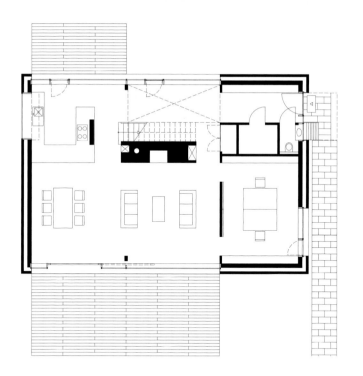

0 | 1   5 m

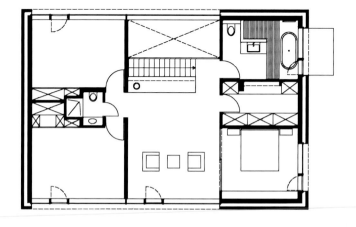

LUP30

Thomas Hillig
Architect

year	2002
collaborators	Hartmut Falkenberg
photos	Jörg F. Müller
site	www.hillig-architekt.de

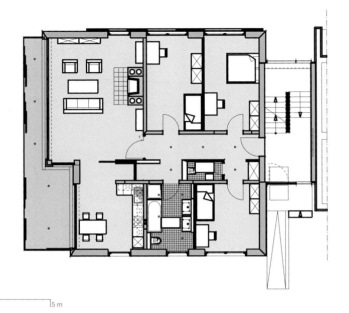

0   1   5 m   0

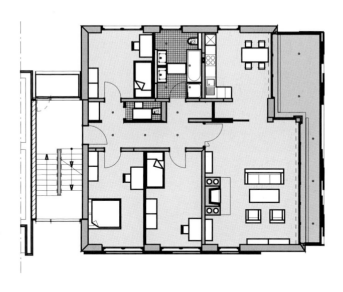

+ 1

0   1   5 m

Ritter House

Thomas Hillig
Architect

year	2002-2004
address	Oberseestraße 48
photos	Thomas Hillig
site	www.hillig-architekt.de

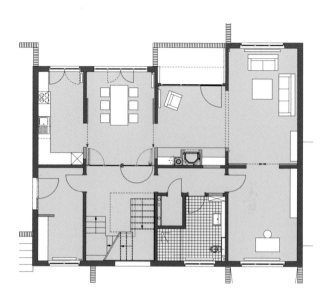

0

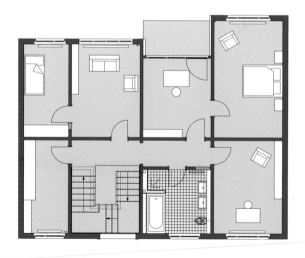

+ 1

Building in Gormannstraße

HSH
Hoyer Schindele Hirschmüller Architecture

year	2009
address	Gormannstraße 8
collaborators	team HSH: Harald Schindele, Markus Hirschmüller, Florian Hoyer and Marcus Schröger, Hille Bekic, Anja Koch, Yoichi Osaki, David Ruic; engineering office Unterberg
photos	Tomek Kwiatosz
site	www.hsharchitektur.de

0 1   5 m

+ 1

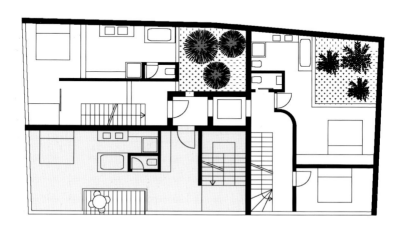

+ 2

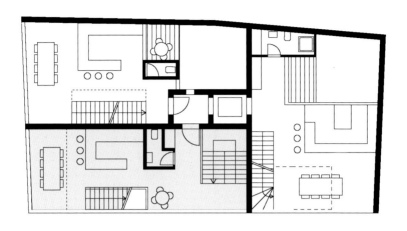

+ 3

0 |1 |5 m

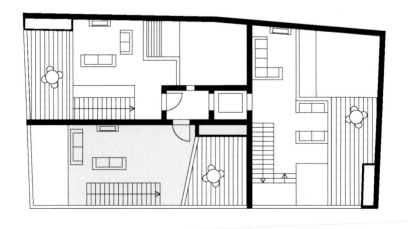

+ 4

Penthouse VII

Jp Studio, Leinweber Architekten

year	2009
address	Lindauer Straße 7
photos	Costa Picadas / Photo for Press
site	www.leinweber-architekten.de

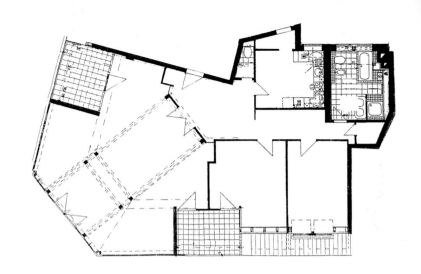

0   2   5 m

e_3

Kaden Klingbeil
Architekten

year	2008
address	Esmarchstraße 3
photos	Bernd Borchard
site	www.kaden-klingbeil.de

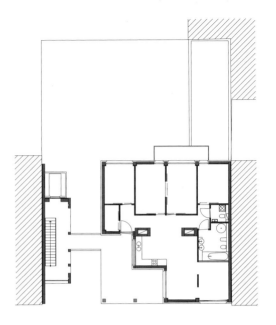

+ 1

0   2   5 m

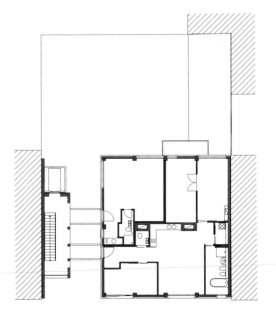

+ 2

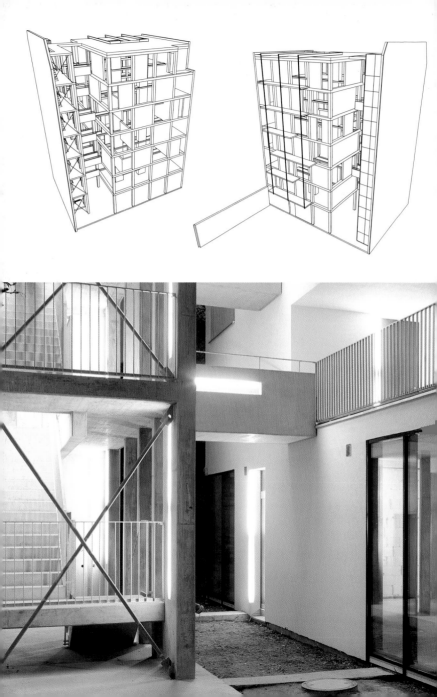

haus160plus

kleyer.koblitz. architekten, Julia Bergmann

year	2005
address	14612 Falkensee
photos	Thorsten Klapsch
site	www.kklf.de

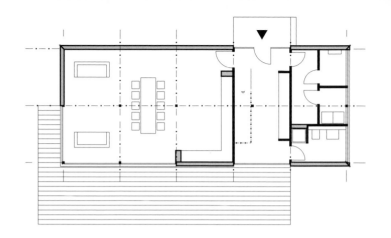

0   1   3 m

0

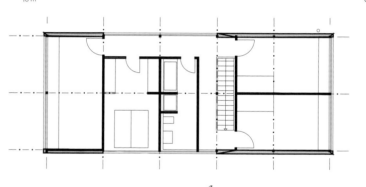

+ 1

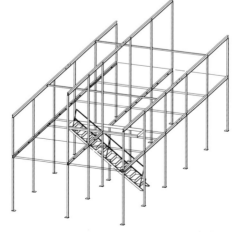

168

Smac House

kleyer.koblitz. architekten, Julia Bergmann

year	2008
address	Potzdam
photos	Thorsten Klapsch
site	www.kklf.de

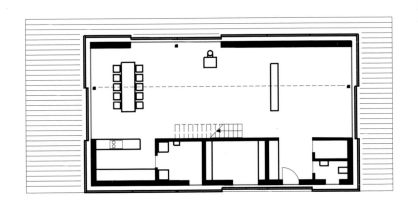

0 1   3 m

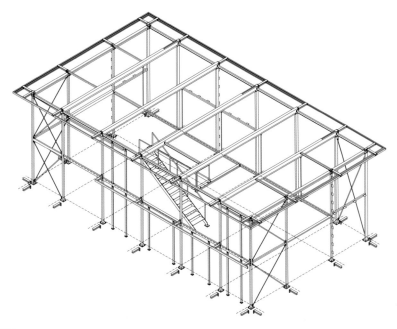

New Apartment Building in Lychener Straße

Kny & Weber Architekten

year	2008
address	Lychener Straße 59
photos	Gerhard Zwickert
site	www.kny-weber.de

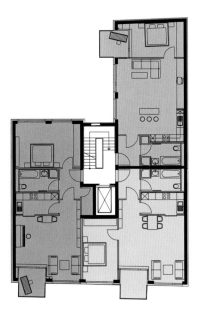

0 2 5 m

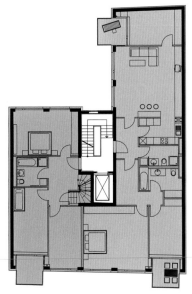

Two Apartment Buildings

Maedebach & Redeleit Architekten

year	2000
address	Riemeisterstraße 29-31
collaborators	J. Kellermann, A. Scholz
photos	Werner Huthmacher
site	www.maedebach-redeleit.de

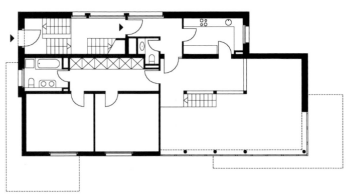

0   2   5 m

0

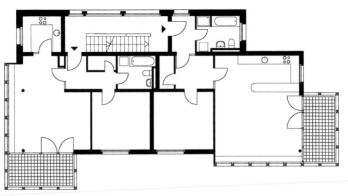

+ 1

0 2 5 m

Residence
Dichter D48

Müller-Stüler und
Höll Architekten

year	2001
address	Dünkelbergsteig 4B
photos	Anita Back
site	www.msh-architekten.de

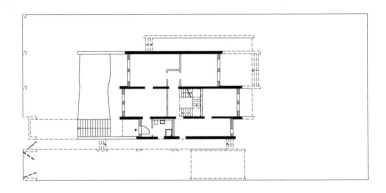

0

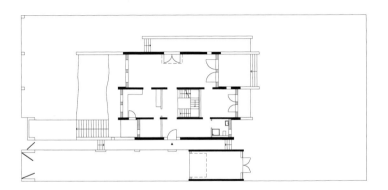

+ 1

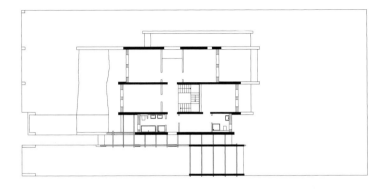

210

0 2 5 m

+ 2

Gable-façaded Buildings

Nägeliarchitekten

year	2006
photos	Mathias Abendthum
site	www.naegeliarchitekten.de

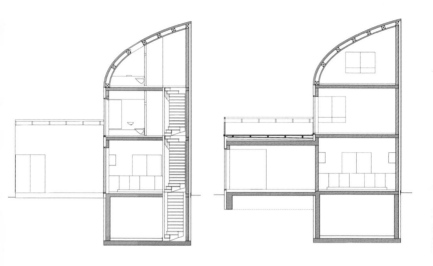

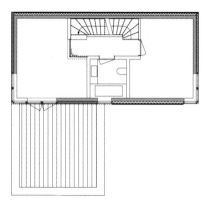

+ 1

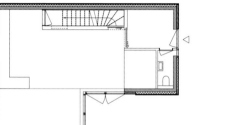

+ 2

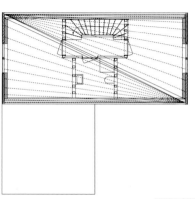

0 1   5 m   + 3

Housing in Sulzaer Straße

Nägeliarchitekten

year	2009
address	Sulzaer Straße
photos	Johanna Diehl
site	www.naegeliarchitekten.de

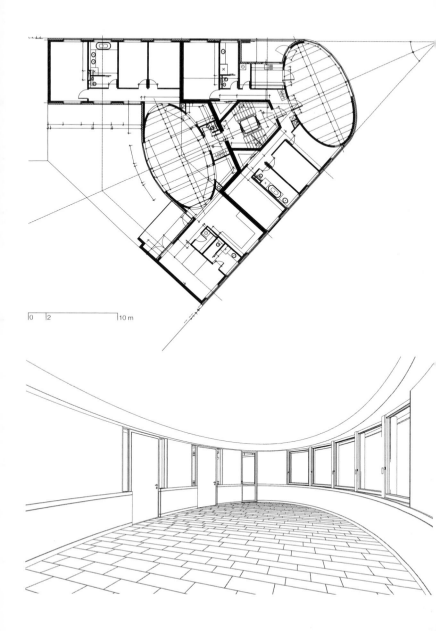

Townhouse
P15

NALBACH + NALBACH

Johanne Nalbach

year	2005-2008
address	Caroline-Von-Humbold-Weg 32
photos	Tobias Wille
site	www.nalbach-architekten.de

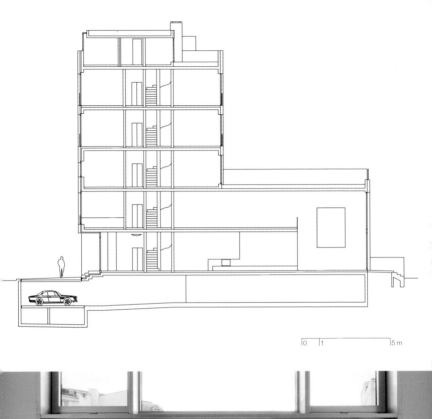

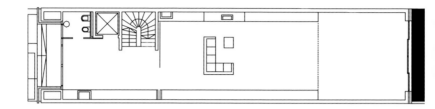

0

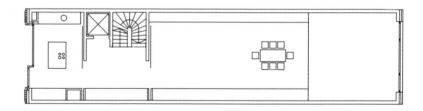

+ 1

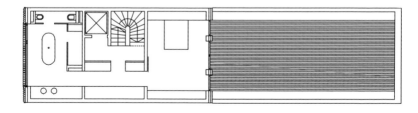

0 1   5 m   + 2

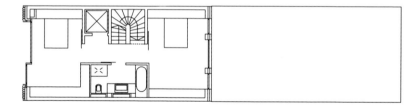

+ 3

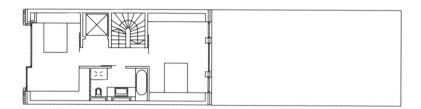

+ 4

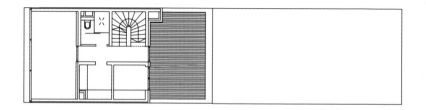

0 1   5 m

Atriumhaus III

Olfearchitektur - Hans-Henninq Olfe

year	2005
photos	Olfearchitektur, Christian Gahl
site	www.olfearchitektur.de

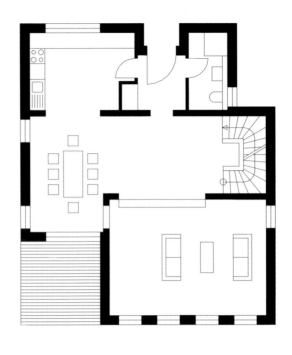

0

1 5 m 0

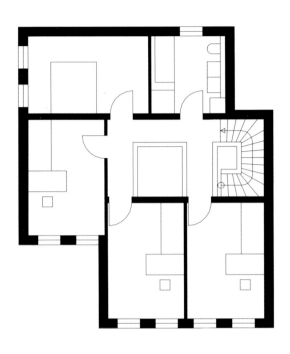

+ 1

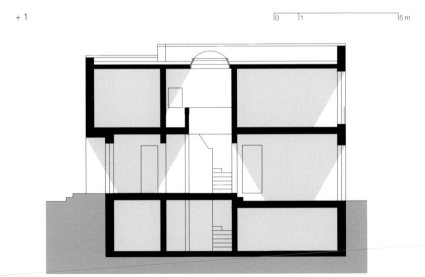

Enlargement and Construction of a New Penthouse

OttoMetzner. Architekt.

year	2003-2004
address	Giesebrechtstraße 5
photos	Costa Picadas / Photo for Press
site	www.metzner-architekt.de

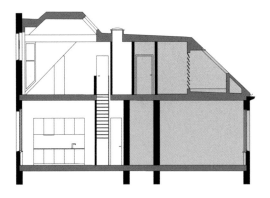

0 1 5 m

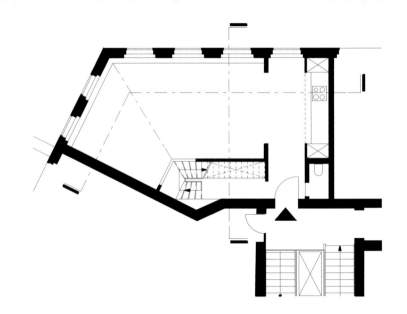

0   1   5 m

+ 4

+ 5

Cantianhaus

Peter Architekten, Michael A. Peter with Wahl und Bauer

year	2001
address	Cantianstraße 11
collaborators	Hans R. Peter, Boris Peter (structural engineers), Ingeborg Peter (gardenplanner)
photos	Klemens Ortmeyer
site	www.wahlundbauer.de

+ 1 / + 2 / + 3

+ 4 / + 5

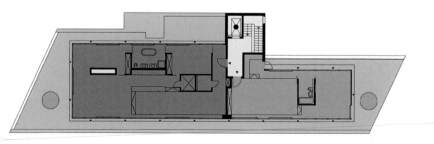

+ 6

0 2   10 m

026 - Residences on Lake Wannsee

Quick Bäckmann Quick + Partner

year	2003
photos	Quick Bäckmann Quick + Partner, Volker Kreidler
site	www.qbq-architekten.de

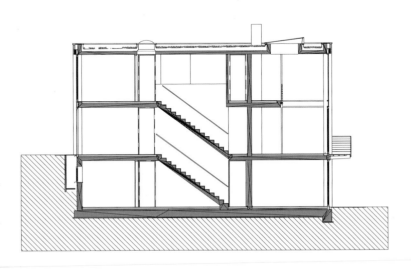

0 2   5 m

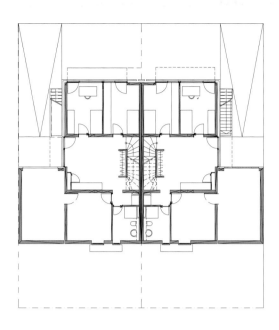

- 1

0   2   5 m

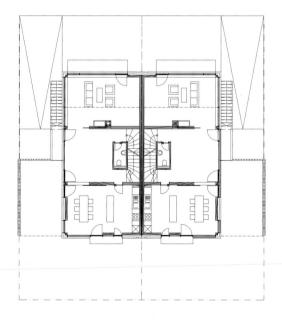

Ten in One – House for the Building Group A52

roedig . schop architekten

year	2005
address	Anklamer Straße 52
photos	Andrea Kroth
site	www.roedig-schop.de

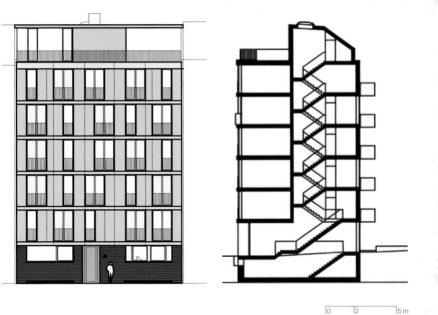

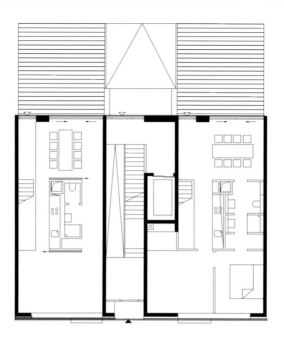

0 2 5 m

Apartment and Office Building

Schlosser Lamborelle

year	2001-2006
address	Elisabethkirchstraße
photos	Stefan Müller
site	www.schlosserlamborelle.com

0 2 5 m

+ 1

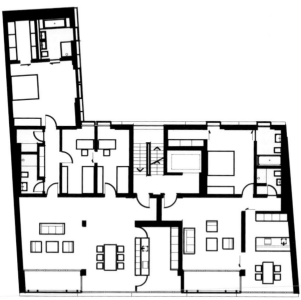

0 2 5 m

Lofthouse

Schlosser
Lamborelle

year	2005
address	Schröderstraße 8
collaborators	Ringo Offermann, Kathrin Schreiber, Daniela Fischer
photos	Christian Gahl, Stefan Müller, Ulrich Schwarz
site	www.schlosserlamborelle.com

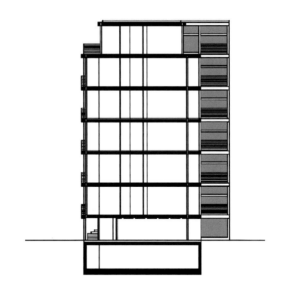

0 2   10 m

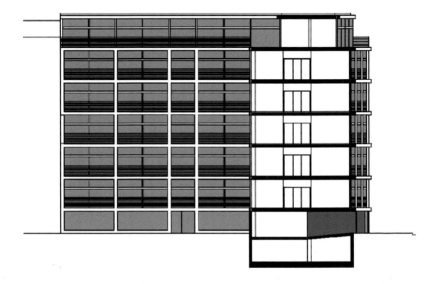

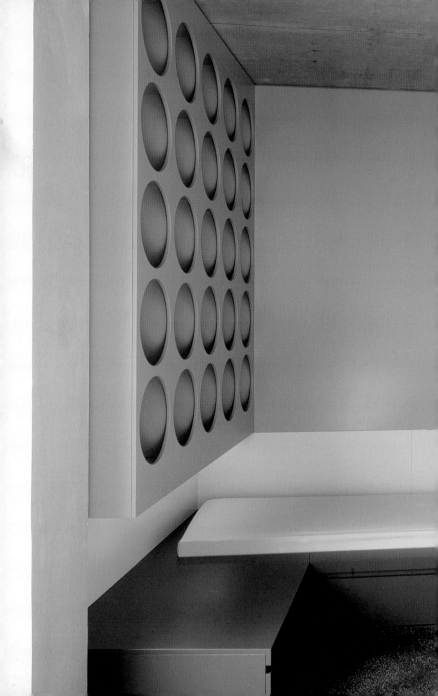

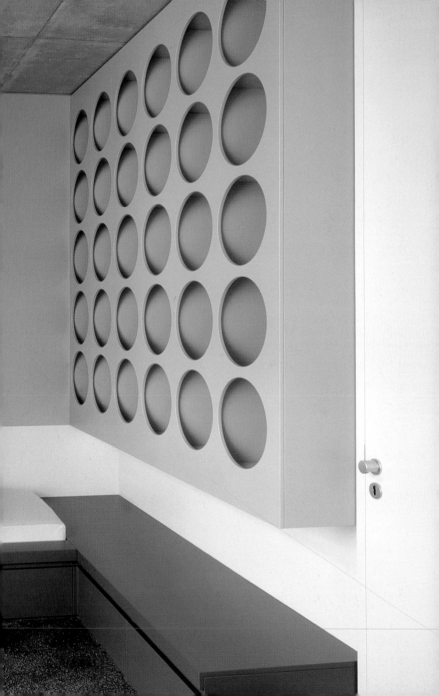

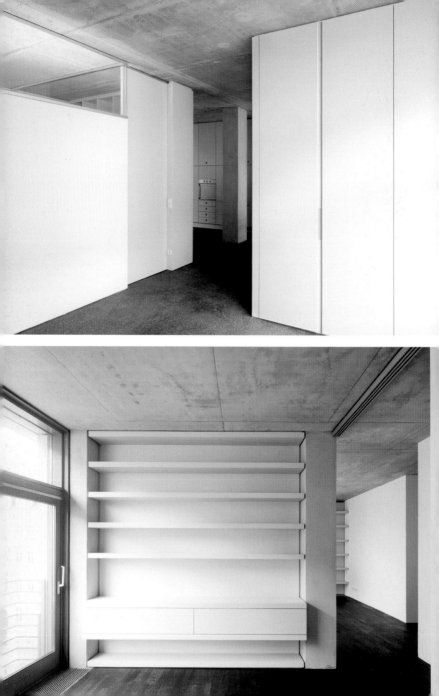

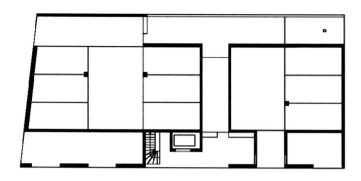

0

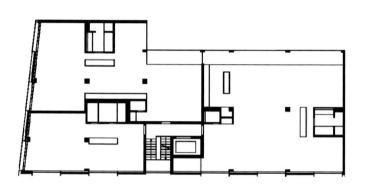

+ 1

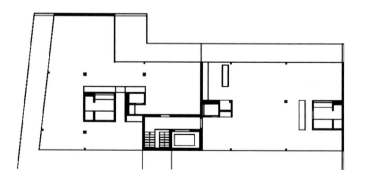

0 2 10 m + 6

Two Detached Residences in Majakowskiring

Architekturbüro Schmid

year	2001-2004
address	Majakowskiring 67/69
collaborators	Franziska Hutter
photos	Ulrich Schwarz
site	www.arch-schmid.de

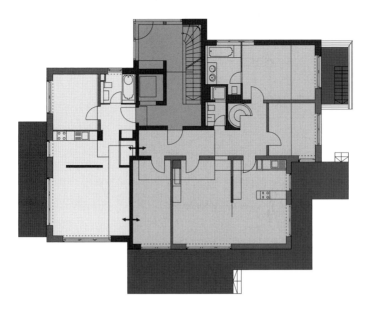

0

0 2 5 m

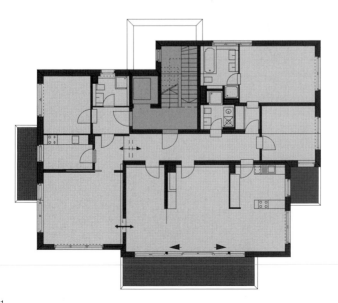

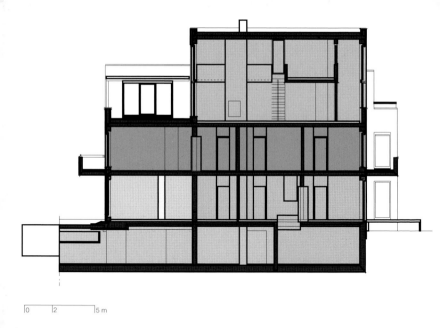

2 families
1 house

Straub Beutin
Architekten - Silke
Straub, Olaf Beutin

year	2001
address	Kreutzerweg 28
photos	Andrea Kroth
site	www.straubbeutin.de

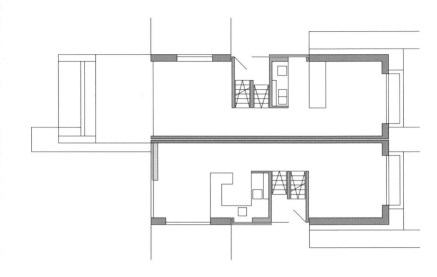

0   2   5 m

0

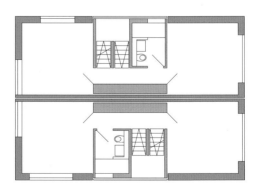

+ 1

Pappelallee 21 A

BUSMANN+HABERER, Stefan Tebroke, Carlo Calderan

year	2008
address	Pappelallee 21 A
photos	Werner Huthmacher
site	www.busmann-haberer.de

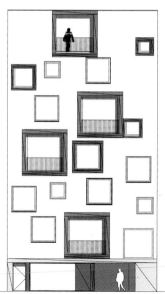

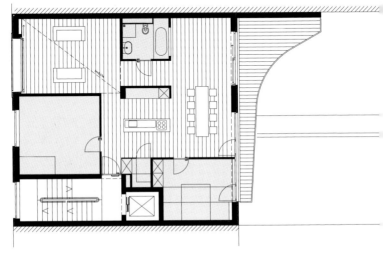

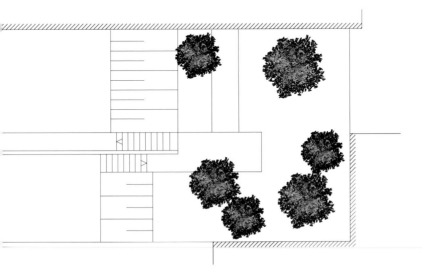

0 | 2 | 5 m

Residential Building Tsingas

Helm Westhaus Architekten

year	2006
address	Majakowskiring 44
photos	Florian Profitlich
site	www.helmwesthaus.de

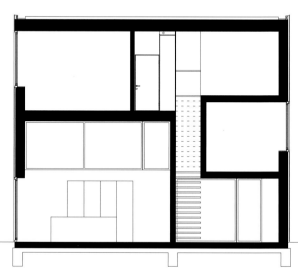

0 | 1 | 3 m

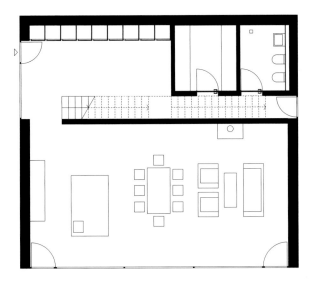

0

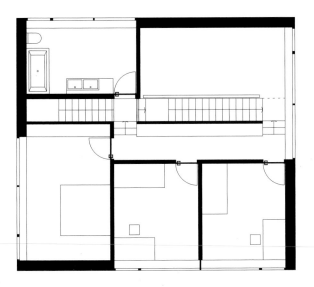

+ 2

Apartment and Office New Building

Zanderroth Architekten

Sascha Zander, Christian Roth

year	2007
address	Linienstraße 87
photos	Andrea Kroth
site	www.zanderroth.de

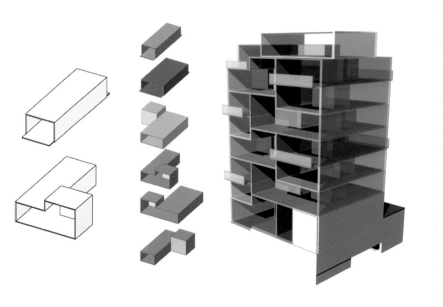

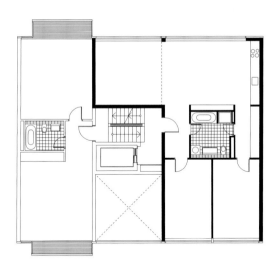

+ 2

0   2   5 m

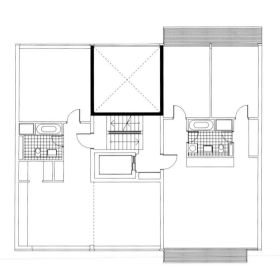

RuSc

Zanderroth
Architekten

Sascha Zander, Christian Roth

year	2007
address	Ruppiner Straße 43, Schönholzer Straße 10 a
collaborators	Guido Neubeck, Annette Schmidt
photos	Andrea Kroth
site	www.zanderroth.de

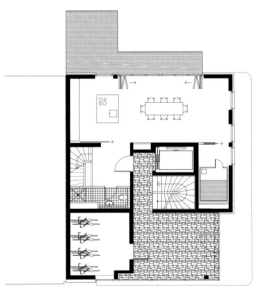

0   1   3 m

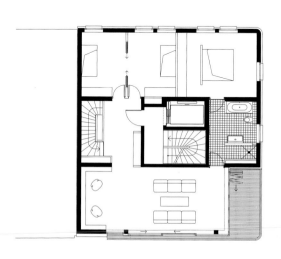

+ 1

0 1 3 m

0 1 3 m

+ 2

+ 3

Federico Ferrari

Architetto laureato presso il Politecnico di Milano e dottorando in urbanistica presso lo IUAV di Venezia, da anni si occupa di critica e storia dell'architettura del secondo Novecento, con particolare riferimento all'area lombarda e alle problematiche inerenti il rapporto fra società di massa e morfologia urbana. Oltre a varie pubblicazioni in campo editoriale e accademico e diverse collaborazioni con la Triennale di Milano, fra cui la co-curatela della mostra *Casa per Tutti* nel 2008, è collaboratore di "Domus" e del "Giornale dell'Architettura".

Federico Ferrari

An architect qualified at Milan Polytechnic and studying for his doctorate in urban planning at IUAV in Venice, for years he has been involved in architectural criticism and history of the late twentieth century, with particular reference to the Lombardy area and the problems inherent in the rapport between mass society and urban morphology. As well as various publications in the editorial and academic field and numerous collaborations with the Milan Triennale, including the joint curatorship of the exhibition Casa per Tutti *in 2008, he collaborates with* Domus *and* Il Giornale dell'Architettura.

Printed in Italy
by 24 ORE Cultura, Milan
April 2010